Fred the Chaffinch

The History of Farming

Text © John Miles
Illustrations © Barry Robson

First published in August 2016
by
Langford Press, 32 Eastfield,
Narborough, Kings Lynn,
Norfolk PE32 1SS
www.langford-press.co.uk

A CIP Record for this book is
available from the British Library
ISBN 978-1-904078-77-7

Designed by MRM Graphics Ltd
Printed in Spain under the supervision
of MRM Graphics Ltd, Winslow

VINE
HOUSE
FARM

bird
foods

Wild Bird Food
Direct from our farm
www.vinehousefarm.co.uk

Fred the Chaffinch sponsored by
Vine House Farm Ltd

Fred the Chaffinch

by John Miles
and
artwork by Barry Robson

Myweebooks

Langford Press

Fred the Chaffinch

Fred is born in a hawthorn bush in a nest built by his mother.
She has woven grass roots in a fork of the bush between the
prickly branches and added moss, feathers and even spiders' silk.
The nest is a deep cup with five eggs. She has incubated them
for fifteen days until Fred cuts his way out of the egg.
He is totally naked and blind as he joins his brothers
and sisters. His mother lifts off from the nest.
The movement of his dad approaching gives
the signal for their long thin necks to
stretch up for their first food consisting
of easily digested insects.

In a few days the eyes open so Fred can actually see who is coming in with food. Feathers start to grow through his naked skin. The nest is well camouflaged in the hawthorn with the bush full of leaves in summer. Old flower heads are turning to berries after being pollinated by insects attracted by the sweet nectar offered by the flowers. The bush is part of a hedge separating fields on an arable farm; a broad strip of wild flowers and grasses divides the hedge from the crop in the field. This provides most of the food - insects in the summer and weed seed and grain in the winter - for Fred's dad and mum.

The name 'chaffinch' comes from the fact the birds were commonly found around humans and grain. As humans developed from 'hunter gathers' (killing wild animals and gathering wild berries to feed themselves) to farmers (rearing their own animals and growing their own food), grain, a large grass seed, became a staple diet.

To extract the grain from the sheaves (stems) the plants were beaten on a flat stone. Both the grain and the chaff would fall off and here the chaffinch would come to eat the waste and get its name!

Records of the birds date back to early man when remains of chaffinches were found in archaeological digs when modern historians were finding out about the past.

Remains of several species of finches including chaffinch were found in a cave called 'Ossom's Eyrie' in the Peak District.

Some remains have been dated to nearly 5,000 years old. 'Eyrie' means the nest of the golden eagle.

Some of the first paintings of the chaffinch appeared in Roman Italy at a site called Pompeii. These are found on mosaics. Mosaics are created by assembling small pieces of coloured glass, stone, or other material, either on a wall or especially on a floor of a building or house. Pompeii is famous for its volcano called Mount Vesuvius which covered the town with ash,

helping to save its mosaics for us to find in modern times. Three cock chaffinches are found on a mosaic here in Pompeii which will be identical to Fred by the time he moults his teenage feathers into adult plumage by next spring!

As farming methods progressed, instead of cutting the grain by hand
using a sickle or scythe, machinery took over with a horse-drawn binder
and the field was stooked with sheaves. When the grain was needed it
was taken to the farm where a new machine called a threshing machine

was used to separate the grain from the stalks. Here again, flocks of chaffinches and other finches and buntings were drawn to this plentiful supply of waste which included weed seed grown up with the grain.

Many of these weed seeds were left on the ground not only in the farm yard but also out in the field. The field, after the grain was removed was called stubble as the hard old stems of the grain were cut close to the ground leaving a prickly covering. These weed seeds were in the soil and

would appear year after year creating a wonderful colour especially of red poppies and yellow corn marigolds. Many chaffinches would use these fields in winter to gather the fallen seed and lost grain for food, as insects were no longer available to most birds remaining in Britain for the winter.

Horses were replaced by tractors and binders by combine harvesters.

These new machines carried out the entire process, taking away the need for the threshing machine and so bringing the grain straight to the farm.

It is stored away to prevent predators feeding on it and so leaves the chaffinch with less food around the farm.

Back in the field further development means that even the stubble and weeds are under threat.

The grain is planted in the autumn and winter which means the stubble is ploughed up to bury the seed and waste grain, leaving bare soil before the new grain is planted.

Modern technology has also allowed the farmer to use sprays which kill the weed seed before it can develop and grow. The fields now do not often have that glow of reds and yellows of the wild flowers. Instead it is a single colour of the developing grain.

This has pushed the chaffinch even more to the boundaries of the field; the hedgerow and the edge of the field are often the only places to find food both in summer and winter.

Even the hedge itself has been under attack. With bigger machinery and demand for more food from a growing population, many hedgerows have been pulled out to make bigger fields to accommodate the machinery. More acres/hectares of land are created to grow more grain.
This has meant less food and fewer nest sites for chaffinches and other birds normally associated with the farm.

B ROBSON '15

Even many hedges have had their hearts cut out of them with modern hedge cutters called flails. These smash branches and stems leaving an ugly mess with little cover left for the chaffinch, making them vulnerable to predation.

This is where Fred has come up trumps. His parents are bringing him up on an organic farm with fields free of chemicals. In addition, spring planting takes place and there are broad hedgerows full of wide field edges. What a lucky bird! No wonder he is out of the nest in fourteen days.
He has fledged and uses the cover of the hedge to keep well away from predators.
He does not have the pink breast like his dad but looks more like his mum with an olive brown back and is duller all round; he blends in with his surroundings.

B ROBSON '15

The full plumage will come next spring when he too will be singing his song to attract a mate (female). This song is a warning to other males about how much land, or territory, is being held by each male chaffinch.

The bigger the area of land the more potential food is available to feed the adult birds and their brood of young like Fred and his brothers and sisters.

Autumn provides an extra food in the form of beech mast. Beech mast is the seed of the beech tree. In some years the trees drop lots of mast which is like a small nut in a hairy shell. This can bring thousands of chaffinches from Europe flying over the North Sea to join Fred and his family. Along with them will come a close relative, the brambling. They are a similar size but have a distinctive white rump (bottom) whereas that of a chaffinch is grey-green with their distinctive white wing bar. The brambling has a lot of black and orange in its plumage but less white on the wing. It is the bill of the chaffinch which determines the type of winter food it can eat.

The finches were made famous by a man called Darwin who wrote a book called "The Origin of Species". It is based on the bill shapes and sizes of finches found on different islands in the Galapagos archipelago in the Pacific Ocean. This confirmed that species evolved over millions of years.

He could have used the finches in Britain with their mixed bills ranging from the large hawfinch to the minute twite. Fred's bill is in the middle range being able to tackle the beech mast but not the stone (seed) of the cherry tree.

Fred must stay in his small family group and learn the alarm calls. 'Pink' is the main call for telling other chaffinches to stay together. A loud 'pink, pink' tells of danger which means either to hide or to fly away close together.

Fred better not get it wrong! You only get one chance when it is a cat on a farm or a sparrowhawk coming in low across the ground to flush (disperse) temporarily the flock.

As autumn approaches many families join together to make larger flocks. These flocks can vary in number from 15 to 100 birds.

Name the Finch:

Select from: Crossbill, Bullfinch, Hawfinch, Twite, Chaffinch and Siskin.

Fred will have to learn both from his parents and from the flock to make it through to the spring. Then he too can create a territory of land to call his own and find a mate to allow him to have his own chicks. Future chaffinches will continue to enjoy this farm.

Present books in the same series:

Kitty the Toon, Screamer the Swift, Gowk the Cuckoo,
Horace the Peregrine, and Mavis the Song Thrush

Forthcoming Titles:

Belle the Barn Owl and Henry the Hen Harrier

Our Sponsors:

Vine House Farm is Lincolnshire's wild bird food specialist.
We offer a wide range of high quality wild bird food, bird feeders and accessories. We grow as much of our bird seed as possible on the farm, and every sale supports the work of The Wildlife Trusts